ADULT-KID COMMUNICATION JOURNAL

To: Blake
I hope this book
adds value to your
life. I Love you!
Hope you know that!
– [illegible] #22

DISCLAIMER:
The information provided in this book is intended for general informational and educational purposes only. This book does not constitute personalized medical or psychological advice, diagnosis, or treatment.

Readers should not use the content of this book as a substitute for professional judgment or as a replacement for individualized advice from a qualified mental health or medical professional. Always consult with a licensed professional for advice tailored to your specific circumstances.

Always seek the advice of a qualified health care provider with any questions you may have regarding a medical or psychological condition. Never disregard professional or mental health advice or delay seeking it because of something you have read in this book.

The use of this book does not establish a therapeutic or professional relationship between the reader and the author. The author disclaims any liability for actions taken or not taken based on the information presented in this book.

First Edition.

Smiley's Publishing
Seattle, WA

Design: Liz Mrofka, What If? Publishing

ISBN: 979-8-9922146-0-4

ADULT-KID COMMUNICATION JOURNAL

STRENGTHEN RELATIONSHIPS, CHANGE GENERATIONAL COMMUNICATION AND ENCOURAGE SAFE CONVERSATIONS

GERALD SMILEY

Smiley's Publishing

DEDICATION

To my parents, for teaching me the value of open communication and the strength it can bring to relationships.

To my wife, for your unwavering support and belief in the power of family bonds.

To my coaches, for showing me how connection and guidance can shape lives.

And to my children, for inspiring me to find ways to bring families closer together and create better ways to communicate effectively.

This book is for all of you—thank you for helping me see the impact of meaningful communication and to view communication from different lenses.

"Speak to me and I may forget.
Show me and I might remember.
Include me and I will understand!"

—Gerald Smiley

ACKNOWLEDGMENTS

I want to take a moment to express my deepest gratitude and appreciation for the incredible team at What If Publishing. Your dedication to your craft is nothing short of extraordinary. From start to finish, your meticulous attention to detail, boundless creativity, and unwavering professionalism have truly shone through.

You've made every step of this journey seamless and enjoyable, with your clear communication and prompt, reliable service. It's rare to find a team that not only brings your vision to life but elevates it beyond what you could have imagined.

Thank you for taking my journal and turning it into something truly special. Your hard work and passion for what you do have made a dream come true, and I'm so grateful to have partnered with you on this project. Thank you for everything!

TABLE OF CONTENTS

PREFACE

The Power of Communication: Building Bridges, Not Walls

WHY COMMUNICATION IS IMPORTANT

Communication is the foundation of every relationship we have—whether it's with our family, friends, colleagues, or even ourselves. It is the tool that allows us to express our thoughts, emotions, and needs. Without effective communication, misunderstandings grow, conflicts linger, and connections weaken.

Think about the last time you felt unheard or misunderstood. That feeling of frustration or isolation? That's what happens when communication breaks down. On the other hand, when someone truly listens to us, acknowledges our emotions, and engages in a meaningful exchange, we feel validated, safe, and connected. Good communication isn't just about talking; it's about being heard, understood, and valued.

THE HEALTH BENEFITS OF COMMUNICATION

Beyond improving relationships, communication has a direct impact on our well-being. When we express ourselves openly, we release stress and reduce emotional burdens. Bottling up emotions can lead to anxiety, depression, and even physical health issues like high blood pressure and weakened immune function.

Studies show that people who have strong communication skills and deep social connections tend to live longer and experience less stress. Expressing emotions in a healthy way can help prevent resentment, anger, and mental exhaustion. Additionally, having meaningful conversations boosts dopamine and oxytocin—chemicals in the brain responsible for happiness and bonding.

When we communicate effectively, we not only strengthen relationships but also improve our overall quality of life.

THE IMPORTANCE OF MEANINGFUL CONNECTIONS

We live in a world that thrives on quick messages, social media updates, and surface-level conversations. But deep, meaningful connections are what truly nourish us. Real connections happen when we communicate openly, listen without judgment, and show up for each other emotionally.

Why do meaningful connections matter? Because we are wired for connection. From the moment we are born, we seek love, validation, and understanding. When we form strong relationships based on trust and communication, we create a support system that helps us navigate life's challenges.

Think about the people in your life who make you feel truly seen and heard. These are the relationships that provide comfort, strength, and motivation. And at the heart of those relationships is communication—the ability to share honestly and vulnerably.

TIPS FOR BETTER COMMUNICATION (EVEN WHEN IT'S HARD)

There will be times when communication feels difficult—whether due to fear, past trauma, or emotional exhaustion. But improving your ability to communicate can transform your relationships and overall well-being. Here are some practical tips:

1. Listen to Understand, Not to Respond

Many people listen just to prepare their next response rather than truly hearing the other person. Active listening means focusing on the speaker, making eye contact, and absorbing what they're saying before forming a reply.

2. Be Honest but Kind

Honesty is essential in communication, but delivery matters. Instead of saying, "You never listen to me," try, "I feel unheard when I try to share my thoughts." This shifts the conversation from blame to expressing feelings.

3. Use 'I' Statements Instead of 'You' Statements

Saying "You always ignore me" can sound accusatory and make the other person defensive. Instead, try: "I feel hurt when I don't get a response." This approach fosters understanding rather than conflict.

4. Be Open to Difficult Conversations

Avoiding hard topics doesn't make problems disappear—it allows resentment to grow. Having open and honest discussions, even when uncomfortable, strengthens relationships.

5. Watch Your Body Language

Nonverbal communication—like facial expressions, tone of voice, and posture—can sometimes say more than words. Maintain eye contact, avoid crossing your arms, and use a calm tone to show you're engaged and open.

6. Take a Pause When Emotions Run High

If a conversation gets too heated, take a break before saying something you'll regret. A simple, "I need a moment to gather my thoughts," can prevent unnecessary arguments and lead to a more productive discussion.

7. Ask Clarifying Questions

If you're unsure about what someone means, ask instead of assuming. Saying, "Can you help me understand what you mean?" prevents misunderstandings and shows that you care about their perspective.

8. Be Willing to Apologize

Apologizing isn't a sign of weakness—it's a sign of emotional maturity. If you've hurt someone with your words, acknowledge it and take responsibility. A sincere "I'm sorry" can heal wounds and rebuild trust.

9. Know When to Walk Away

Not every conversation will be productive, and not every relationship is worth holding onto. If someone refuses to communicate in a healthy way, it's okay to set boundaries and protect your peace.

10. Practice Regularly

Like any skill, communication improves with practice. Make an effort to have deeper conversations, express yourself honestly, and listen with intent. The more you do it, the easier it becomes.

FINAL THOUGHTS

Communication is more than just talking—it's connecting, understanding, and building trust. It has the power to strengthen relationships, improve mental and physical health, and create a more fulfilling life.

The next time you hesitate to express yourself or struggle to listen to someone else, remember this: Every conversation is an opportunity to build a bridge instead of a wall. Choose to communicate with honesty, empathy, and openness. It could change everything.

> "Good communication is the bridge between confusion and clarity."
>
> —Nat Turner

OUR FOREVER AGREEMENT

We, [Kid's name ____] and

[Adult's Name ____],

promise to always support, respect, and be there for each other. As a team, we will work together to grow, learn, and face life's challenges with love and understanding. This is our official agreement to always be a great team!

OUR PROMISES TO EACH OTHER:

1. **We promise to listen to each other with open hearts and open minds.**

- Example: "I will listen when you share your feelings, even if I don't fully understand at first."

2. **We promise to always be honest with each other, even when it's hard.**

- Example: "If something is bothering me, I will talk about it instead of holding it inside."

3. **We promise to support each other's dreams and goals.**

- Example: "I will encourage you to go after your dreams, no matter how big or small."

4. **We promise to work through tough moments with kindness and patience.**

- Example: "If we have a disagreement, we will take a deep breath and talk it out."

5. **We promise to make time for fun, laughter, and special moments together.**

- Example: "We will create fun traditions, like game nights or adventure days."

6. **We promise to always remind each other how important and loved we are.**

- Example: "Even on busy days, we will find ways to show we care."

OUR SPECIAL GOALS

(Write a few things you want to achieve together!)

1.

2.

3.

OUR SIGNATURE MOVE
(OUR SPECIAL HANDSHAKE OR SYMBOL)

(Create a handshake, a fun phrase, or a symbol that represents your team!)

- Example: "Whenever we say 'Team [Last Name] Forever!' we know we have each other's back."

Our Signatures:

✍ [Kid's Name]: ______________________________

✍ [Adult's Name]: ______________________________

Date: ______________________________

This is our forever agreement to be a strong, loving, and supportive team—no matter what!

Lean Into Each Other

This next section is where I want you to lean into each other. Take a deep breath, slow down, and be fully present. This is your space—a space to be open, honest, and real with one another. No judgment. No distractions. Just the two of you.

Before setting this journal down, take a moment to talk. Really talk. Share your authentic answers to these questions. Be authentically you! Listen with the intention of understanding, not just responding.

Connection doesn't happen by accident. It happens when two people decide to be vulnerable with one another, to let their guards down, and to create a space where both feel safe to be themselves. This journal is not just a place for writing —it's a tool to deepen your bond.

After spending time in this section, reflect on how you feel. Do you feel lighter? Closer? More understood? Let this be a reminder that communication is a bridge, and every conversation strengthens it.

Now, take a moment. Lean in. Be present. This is your space to grow together.

INTRODUCTION

Why I Created This Journal

In today's world, with the constant distractions of technology, the pressures of daily life, busy lives always on the go, and the emotional roller coasters of growing up, communication between adults and kids can easily break down. It's not uncommon for families to feel disconnected even while living under the same roof. This journal was born out of a desire to bridge that gap, to create a tool that helps adults and kids understand one another better, without the noise and the interruptions of our busy lives.

I was once a kid who was constantly misunderstood by my parents and other adults, and I misunderstood my them at times as well. I grew up in a home with constant yelling and screaming, to get your points across if there was a disagreement. I saw my parents communicate that way a lot and others. It was dominating behaviors at each other.

I believe that writing can open doors that conversations sometimes cannot. When emotions are high or words come out the wrong way, sitting down and writing how you feel provides space to reflect, to process, and to communicate in a way that is calm and constructive. This journal offers a simple yet powerful system that helps both adults and kids express their feelings, frustrations, and needs, and work together to solve problems in a peaceful way. Understanding other people's point of view is a skill, that must be practiced.

In a world where devices often divide us, this journal is a way to reconnect, to slow down, and to focus on what really matters: your relationship. By setting aside time to write, reflect, and respond, you create an intentional space to be heard and to hear one another, strengthening your bond and avoiding unnecessary conflicts.

DEEPENING CONNECTION

By writing, reflecting, and engaging in open conversations, you'll create a foundation of trust and support. The more you communicate with honesty and intention, the deeper your relationship will grow and continue to learn each other.

Communication is more than just words—it's how we express love, understanding, and connection. Let this be a space where you celebrate each other, learn each other, and build a stronger connection that lasts a lifetime.

Now, let's walk through how to use this journal effectively.

CHOOSING A HOME FOR YOUR JOURNAL

The success of this journal relies on both the adult and kid being able to access it easily and consistently. This should be a neutral, agreed-upon place in your house or classroom, where the journal will live when it's ready to be read or written in.

SOME IDEAS FOR A GOOD LOCATION:

- A common area, like the living room or kitchen counter, where it can be seen regularly.
- A bookshelf or a side table where both adult and kid can easily leave it after writing.
- A bedroom dresser, in a visible spot but one that respects the privacy of its contents.

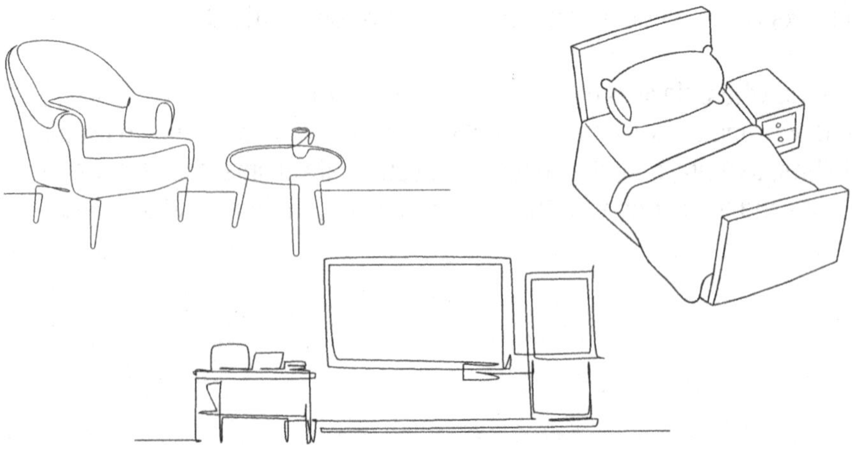

The key is to pick a place that is convenient for both of you—a spot that's easy to access, but not too private that the other person would miss it. When one person has finished their entry, the journal should be returned to this spot, with the green side facing up, signaling that it's ready to be read. By establishing a clear location, you can ensure that the process flows naturally and avoids confusion about when the journal is ready for the next person's turn.

This simple routine can make a world of difference in how you engage with each other.

I hope you enjoy this journey, that I feel will change your lives forever.

> "The most important things in life are the connections you make with others.
>
> —Tom Ford"

"

A true commitment is two souls choosing to grow together—promising to be better, do better, and stand by each other through every storm and every sunrise.

—Gerald Smiley

"

DEEPENING CONVERSATIONS

That Create Clarity and a Safe Space For Each Other

The next pages are a set of deep, thoughtful questions along with example answers for each. These sample responses can serve as inspiration for honest, reflective conversations that build trust and understanding between kids and adults.

Take turns asking each other these questions. Be open and honest about what you choose to share.

KID QUESTION

What was the hardest thing you went through as a kid, and how did you get through it?

- Example Answer: "When I was your age, I lost a really close friend because we moved away. It was really tough, but I learned to keep in touch and also make new friends. It taught me that life changes, but good people stay in your heart."

Do you ever feel pressure to be someone you're not?

ADULT QUESTION

- Example Answer: "Yes, I sometimes feel like I have to act a certain way or like I need to be perfect just to fit in with my friends. It makes me feel like I'm not being my true self."

KID QUESTION

Have you ever felt left out or like you didn't belong or fit in? How did you handle it?

- Example Answer: "Yes, in middle school, I didn't fit in with the popular kids, and that made me feel invisible. I eventually found friends who accepted me for who I was, and that made all the difference."

Have you ever felt left out or like you didn't belong or fit in? How did you handle it or do you need help now?

ADULT QUESTION

- Example Answer: "Yes, in middle school, I didn't fit in with the popular kids, and that made me feel invisible. I eventually found friends who accepted me for who I was, and that made all the difference."

KID QUESTION

What's something you wish you had done differently when you were younger?

- Example Answer: "I wish I had been more confident in myself. I spent too much time worrying about what others thought instead of chasing my own dreams."

Do you feel like I listen to you enough? What could I do better?

ADULT QUESTION

- Example Answer: "Sometimes I feel like my voice gets lost when we're busy. It might help if we set aside a little time just for us to talk without distractions."

KID QUESTION

What's one thing about your childhood that you wish I could experience too?

- Example Answer: "Riding bikes with my friends until the sun went down. We didn't have phones—just adventures."

Has anyone ever made you feel unsafe or uncomfortable?

ADULT QUESTION

- Example Answer: "There was a time when a classmate put their hands on me, and it made me feel very uneasy. I told my teacher about it because I knew I should feel safe at school."

KID QUESTION

What's one thing you wish you could change about yourself?

- Example Answer: "I wish I could learn to be more present in everyday life and not consumed with my telephone."

What's one thing you wish you could change about yourself?

ADULT QUESTION

- Example Answer: "I wish I could be less nervous when I have to speak in front of the class because I really want to share my ideas without fear."

KID QUESTION

Have you ever felt like people don't really understand you?

- Example Answer: "Sometimes I feel like when I talk about my favorite hobbies, my friends don't really get it, and that makes me feel a little alone."

Have you ever felt like people don't really understand you?

ADULT QUESTION

- Example Answer: "Sometimes I feel like when I talk about my feelings, I get shutdown and nobody cares to listen.

KID QUESTION

What's the scariest thing you've ever had to face alone?

- Example Answer: "One time I got lost in a big park during the evening. I felt really scared because I couldn't find my way home, and it taught me how important it is to stick with someone I trust."

If you could apologize to one person, who would it be and why?

ADULT QUESTION

- Example Answer: "I'd apologize to my younger sister for the times I wasn't there for her when she needed me. I regret not being around more during her difficult moments."

KID QUESTION

What's the hardest decision you've ever had to make? And what did you learn?

- Example Answer: "The hardest decision was choosing between playing sports or getting a job, but I learned that sometimes you must choose, even when it feels unfair.

____

____

____

____

____

____

____

Is there something you're struggling with right now but afraid to talk about?

ADULT QUESTION

- Example Answer: "I'm having a hard time with some of my schoolwork, but I'm afraid to say so because I worry my teacher might think I'm not smart. I'm still working on finding the courage to ask for help."

____

____

____

____

____

____

KID QUESTION

Have you ever lost a friendship or a loved one? How did you handle it?

- Example Answer: "Yes, one of my best friends moved away, and I felt really sad about it. I learned that while friendships can change, the memories we make stay with us. I made sure to make time and check on them regularly."

Do you ever feel like you don't have anyone to talk to about your real feelings?

ADULT QUESTION

- Example Answer: "Yes, there have been moments when I've felt isolated despite having many people around me. It's been hard to find someone who truly understands my inner struggles."

KID QUESTION

What's the biggest lesson life has ever taught you the hard way?

- Example Answer: "I learned that vulnerability isn't a weakness but a strength. Opening up, even when it's difficult, has helped me build more meaningful and supportive relationships."

What's one thing that makes you sad, even if no one knows about it?

ADULT QUESTION

- Example Answer: "Sometimes I feel really sad when I see someone being bullied, because it makes me wish that everyone could be kind to one another."

KID QUESTION

What's one thing you're still trying to heal from?

- Example Answer: "I'm still healing from a significant relationship that left me questioning my self-worth. Each day brings a little more healing, even if it doesn't always feel that way."

What is one thing you need more of from me?

ADULT QUESTION

- Example Answer: "I need more time with you. I feel like you're so busy with work and other things, that we barely get to hang out."

HOW TO USE YOUR ADULT-KID JOURNAL

This journal is designed to help you and your adult/kid communicate when emotions are high or when you're feeling frustrated, upset, or need to be heard. It provides a safe space for both of you to express your feelings and work together to find solutions—without arguing, yelling, or interrupting each other.

By using this journal and following the Green Side / Red Side System, you can improve communication, avoid unnecessary arguments, and strengthen your relationship. Writing gives both of you time to think and respond calmly, allowing for more understanding and problem-solving.

HERE'S A SIMPLE GUIDE ON HOW TO USE THE JOURNAL EFFECTIVELY:

1. The Green Side / Red Side System

The journal cover has two colors: Green and Red.

- **Green Side:** When the book is left with the green side facing up, it signals that it's your turn to read and write. The other person has already written their thoughts, and now it's your turn to respond.
- **Red Side:** When the book is left with the red side facing up, it signals that the other person is still writing, or hasn't written yet. You should wait for the green side to face up before reading and responding.

Important Rule: Neither the adult nor the kid should speak about the situation until both have had the opportunity to write in the journal. Communication begins only after both have read and written their entries.

2. When to Use the Journal

- **During Arguments or Frustration:** If emotions are high, and it's difficult to talk without shouting, one of you can suggest using the journal instead of talking. This helps avoid hurtful words and ensures both of you get a chance to be heard.

- **When Feeling Misunderstood:** If one of you feels like you're not being understood in a conversation, pause and decide to write in the journal to express yourself calmly and clearly.
- **As a Regular Check-in:** Even when there's no immediate conflict, you can use the journal to reflect on your relationship, ask questions, or express things you might have trouble saying out loud.

3. Steps for Using the Journal

1. **Turn to the Journal Instead of yelling or screaming:** When things start to get heated, or you feel upset, calmly suggest using the journal. One person can start by flipping the journal to the red side, showing they are going to write first.
2. **Write Down Your Feelings and Needs:** Write about how you're feeling. Be honest, but respectful. Use "I" statements like "I feel upset when . . ." rather than "You make me upset because . . . "
3. **Flip the Book to the Green Side:** Once you've finished writing, place the journal in a spot where the other person can see it, with the green side facing up, letting them know it's their turn to read and respond.
4. **Read, Reflect, and Write Your Response:** The other person should then read what was written, take some time to think, and write their response. They should express their feelings and needs as well, and suggest actions to make things better.
5. **Keep Communication Calm:** Only after both people have written and read each other's thoughts should you come together to discuss what was written. The goal is to communicate calmly and find a solution that works for both of you.

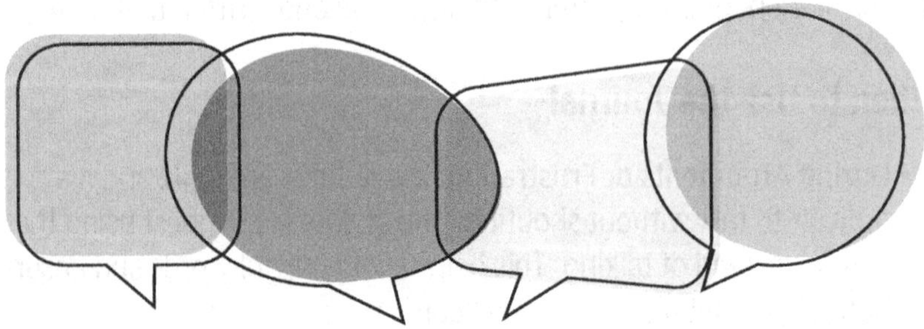

4. Structure for Writing in the Journal

Each time you write, follow this basic structure:

- **How I'm Feeling:** Write about your emotions. Are you frustrated, upset, hurt, or confused? Be specific.
- **What I Need From You:** Tell the other person what you need to feel better. Do you need space, understanding, a change in behavior, or help?
- **What We Can Do Together:** End your entry by suggesting what the two of you can do to improve the situation. It could be setting new rules, spending time together, or simply talking things out after the journal entry.

5. Final Notes on Using the Journal

- **Respect Each Other's Words:** Both the adult and kid should approach this journal with respect for one another's feelings. The journal is a judgment-free space, where both sides can share honestly.
- **Take Time to Cool Down:** If you're really upset, take a few deep breaths before writing. Give yourself a moment to calm down so you can write with a clear mind.
- **Use the Journal Regularly:** This journal doesn't just have to be used during arguments. It can also be a space for celebrating good moments, writing kind messages to each other, or discussing things you may not feel comfortable saying out loud.

ADULT SITUATION________________________________

These words can sometimes be a bridge to opening up, making it easier to share feelings in a way that resonates. Circle a word, or words, that match your feelings currently. This helps who you're communicating with, know where you're coming from in your heart and mind.

Feel-Good Emotions:		**Hard-to-Discuss Feelings:**	
Grateful	Excited	Vulnerable	Resentful
Loved	Confident	Isolated	Unheard
Happy	Supported	Anxious	Trapped
Peaceful	Encouraged	Overwhelmed	Hopeless
Proud	Secure	Insecure	Lonely
Joyful	Hopeful	Misunderstood	Defeated
Appreciated	Inspired	Conflicted	Ashamed

Describe how you're feeling right now. Are you sad, angry, frustrated, worried, or something else? Write about why you're feeling this way.

I'm feeling:

____

____

____

____

____

____

____

____

____

What could my kid do to help?
Maybe you need them to listen, follow a rule, or talk calmly.

What I need from you is:

What things can you both do to solve the problem?
Maybe spend time talking, set up a new rule, or agree on a plan.

One thing we can do together to make things better is:

Do you need advice? **If so, what advice are you looking for?**

KID SITUATION________________________________

These words can sometimes be a bridge to opening up, making it easier to share feelings in a way that resonates. Circle a word, or words, that match your feelings currently. This helps who you're communicating with, know where you're coming from in your heart and mind.

Feel-Good Emotions:		**Hard-to-Discuss Feelings:**	
Grateful	Excited	Vulnerable	Resentful
Loved	Confident	Isolated	Unheard
Happy	Supported	Anxious	Trapped
Peaceful	Encouraged	Overwhelmed	Hopeless
Proud	Secure	Insecure	Lonely
Joyful	Hopeful	Misunderstood	Defeated
Appreciated	Inspired	Conflicted	Ashamed

Describe how you're feeling right now. Are you sad, angry, frustrated, worried, or something else? Write about why you're feeling this way.

I'm feeling:

____

____

____

____

____

____

____

____

____

What could my adult do to help you feel better?
Maybe you need space, a hug, or just for them to listen.

What I need from you is:

What things can you both do to solve the problem?
Maybe spend time talking, set up a new rule, or agree on a plan.

One thing we can do together to make things better is:

Do you need advice? **If so, what advice are you looking for?**

KID REFLECTION SITUATION ____________________

- How I feel about our progress so far is:

____

____

____

____

____

____

- One thing I've learned about my adult/adults is:

____

____

____

____

____

____

- One thing I still need help with is:

____

____

____

____

____

____

SITUATION____

ADULT REFLECTION

- How I feel about our progress so far is:

____
____
____
____
____
____

- One thing I've learned about my kid is:

____
____
____
____
____
____

- One thing we can continue to work on is:

____
____
____
____
____
____

ADULT SITUATION____

These words can sometimes be a bridge to opening up, making it easier to share feelings in a way that resonates. Circle a word, or words, that match your feelings currently. This helps who you're communicating with, know where you're coming from in your heart and mind.

Feel-Good Emotions:		Hard-to-Discuss Feelings:	
Grateful	Excited	Vulnerable	Resentful
Loved	Confident	Isolated	Unheard
Happy	Supported	Anxious	Trapped
Peaceful	Encouraged	Overwhelmed	Hopeless
Proud	Secure	Insecure	Lonely
Joyful	Hopeful	Misunderstood	Defeated
Appreciated	Inspired	Conflicted	Ashamed

Describe how you're feeling right now. Are you sad, angry, frustrated, worried, or something else? Write about why you're feeling this way.

I'm feeling:

____

____

____

____

____

____

____

____

____

What could my kid do to help?
Maybe you need them to listen, follow a rule, or talk calmly.

What I need from you is:

What things can you both do to solve the problem?
Maybe spend time talking, set up a new rule, or agree on a plan.

One thing we can do together to make things better is:

Do you need advice? **If so, what advice are you looking for?**

KID SITUATION____________________________________

These words can sometimes be a bridge to opening up, making it easier to share feelings in a way that resonates. Circle a word, or words, that match your feelings currently. This helps who you're communicating with, know where you're coming from in your heart and mind.

Feel-Good Emotions:		**Hard-to-Discuss Feelings:**	
Grateful	Excited	Vulnerable	Resentful
Loved	Confident	Isolated	Unheard
Happy	Supported	Anxious	Trapped
Peaceful	Encouraged	Overwhelmed	Hopeless
Proud	Secure	Insecure	Lonely
Joyful	Hopeful	Misunderstood	Defeated
Appreciated	Inspired	Conflicted	Ashamed

Describe how you're feeling right now. Are you sad, angry, frustrated, worried, or something else? Write about why you're feeling this way.

I'm feeling:

____

____

____

____

____

____

____

____

____

What could my adult do to help you feel better?
Maybe you need space, a hug, or just for them to listen.

What I need from you is:

What things can you both do to solve the problem?
Maybe spend time talking, set up a new rule, or agree on a plan.

One thing we can do together to make things better is:

Do you need advice? **If so, what advice are you looking for?**

KID REFLECTION SITUATION ______________________________

- How I feel about our progress so far is:

____

____

____

____

____

____

- One thing I've learned about my adult/adults is:

____

____

____

____

____

____

- One thing I still need help with is:

____

____

____

____

____

____

SITUATION____

ADULT REFLECTION

- How I feel about our progress so far is:

____

____

____

____

____

____

- One thing I've learned about my kid is:

____

____

____

____

____

____

- One thing we can continue to work on is:

____

____

____

____

____

____

ADULT SITUATION____

These words can sometimes be a bridge to opening up, making it easier to share feelings in a way that resonates. Circle a word, or words, that match your feelings currently. This helps who you're communicating with, know where you're coming from in your heart and mind.

Feel-Good Emotions:		**Hard-to-Discuss Feelings:**	
Grateful	Excited	Vulnerable	Resentful
Loved	Confident	Isolated	Unheard
Happy	Supported	Anxious	Trapped
Peaceful	Encouraged	Overwhelmed	Hopeless
Proud	Secure	Insecure	Lonely
Joyful	Hopeful	Misunderstood	Defeated
Appreciated	Inspired	Conflicted	Ashamed

Describe how you're feeling right now. Are you sad, angry, frustrated, worried, or something else? Write about why you're feeling this way.

I'm feeling:

____

____

____

____

____

____

____

____

____

What could my kid do to help?
Maybe you need them to listen, follow a rule, or talk calmly.

What I need from you is:

What things can you both do to solve the problem?
Maybe spend time talking, set up a new rule, or agree on a plan.

One thing we can do together to make things better is:

Do you need advice? **If so, what advice are you looking for?**

KID SITUATION ______________________________

These words can sometimes be a bridge to opening up, making it easier to share feelings in a way that resonates. Circle a word, or words, that match your feelings currently. This helps who you're communicating with, know where you're coming from in your heart and mind.

Feel-Good Emotions:		**Hard-to-Discuss Feelings:**	
Grateful	Excited	Vulnerable	Resentful
Loved	Confident	Isolated	Unheard
Happy	Supported	Anxious	Trapped
Peaceful	Encouraged	Overwhelmed	Hopeless
Proud	Secure	Insecure	Lonely
Joyful	Hopeful	Misunderstood	Defeated
Appreciated	Inspired	Conflicted	Ashamed

Describe how you're feeling right now. Are you sad, angry, frustrated, worried, or something else? Write about why you're feeling this way.

I'm feeling:

____

____

____

____

____

____

____

____

____

What could my adult do to help you feel better?
Maybe you need space, a hug, or just for them to listen.

What I need from you is:

What things can you both do to solve the problem?
Maybe spend time talking, set up a new rule, or agree on a plan.

One thing we can do together to make things better is:

Do you need advice? **If so, what advice are you looking for?**

KID REFLECTION SITUATION ________________________________

- How I feel about our progress so far is:

____
____
____
____
____
____

- One thing I've learned about my adult/adults is:

____
____
____
____
____
____

- One thing I still need help with is:

____
____
____
____
____
____

SITUATION________________________________

ADULT REFLECTION

- How I feel about our progress so far is:

____

____

____

____

____

____

- One thing I've learned about my kid is:

____

____

____

____

____

____

- One thing we can continue to work on is:

____

____

____

____

____

____

ADULT SITUATION ____________________

These words can sometimes be a bridge to opening up, making it easier to share feelings in a way that resonates. Circle a word, or words, that match your feelings currently. This helps who you're communicating with, know where you're coming from in your heart and mind.

Feel-Good Emotions:		Hard-to-Discuss Feelings:	
Grateful	Excited	Vulnerable	Resentful
Loved	Confident	Isolated	Unheard
Happy	Supported	Anxious	Trapped
Peaceful	Encouraged	Overwhelmed	Hopeless
Proud	Secure	Insecure	Lonely
Joyful	Hopeful	Misunderstood	Defeated
Appreciated	Inspired	Conflicted	Ashamed

Describe how you're feeling right now. Are you sad, angry, frustrated, worried, or something else? Write about why you're feeling this way.

I'm feeling:

____

____

____

____

____

____

____

____

____

What could my kid do to help?
Maybe you need them to listen, follow a rule, or talk calmly.

What I need from you is:

What things can you both do to solve the problem?
Maybe spend time talking, set up a new rule, or agree on a plan.

One thing we can do together to make things better is:

Do you need advice? **If so, what advice are you looking for?**

KID SITUATION____

These words can sometimes be a bridge to opening up, making it easier to share feelings in a way that resonates. Circle a word, or words, that match your feelings currently. This helps who you're communicating with, know where you're coming from in your heart and mind.

Feel-Good Emotions:		**Hard-to-Discuss Feelings:**	
Grateful	Excited	Vulnerable	Resentful
Loved	Confident	Isolated	Unheard
Happy	Supported	Anxious	Trapped
Peaceful	Encouraged	Overwhelmed	Hopeless
Proud	Secure	Insecure	Lonely
Joyful	Hopeful	Misunderstood	Defeated
Appreciated	Inspired	Conflicted	Ashamed

Describe how you're feeling right now. Are you sad, angry, frustrated, worried, or something else? Write about why you're feeling this way.

I'm feeling:

____

____

____

____

____

____

____

____

____

What could my adult do to help you feel better?
Maybe you need space, a hug, or just for them to listen.

What I need from you is:

What things can you both do to solve the problem?
Maybe spend time talking, set up a new rule, or agree on a plan.

One thing we can do together to make things better is:

Do you need advice? **If so, what advice are you looking for?**

KID REFLECTION

SITUATION ______________________________

- How I feel about our progress so far is:

____
____
____
____
____
____

- One thing I've learned about my adult/adults is:

____
____
____
____
____
____

- One thing I still need help with is:

____
____
____
____
____
____

SITUATION____

ADULT REFLECTION

- How I feel about our progress so far is:

____

____

____

____

____

____

- One thing I've learned about my kid is:

____

____

____

____

____

____

- One thing we can continue to work on is:

____

____

____

____

____

____

ADULT SITUATION________________________________

These words can sometimes be a bridge to opening up, making it easier to share feelings in a way that resonates. Circle a word, or words, that match your feelings currently. This helps who you're communicating with, know where you're coming from in your heart and mind.

Feel-Good Emotions:		**Hard-to-Discuss Feelings:**	
Grateful	Excited	Vulnerable	Resentful
Loved	Confident	Isolated	Unheard
Happy	Supported	Anxious	Trapped
Peaceful	Encouraged	Overwhelmed	Hopeless
Proud	Secure	Insecure	Lonely
Joyful	Hopeful	Misunderstood	Defeated
Appreciated	Inspired	Conflicted	Ashamed

Describe how you're feeling right now. Are you sad, angry, frustrated, worried, or something else? Write about why you're feeling this way.

I'm feeling:

____

____

____

____

____

____

____

____

____

What could my kid do to help?
Maybe you need them to listen, follow a rule, or talk calmly.

What I need from you is:

What things can you both do to solve the problem?
Maybe spend time talking, set up a new rule, or agree on a plan.

One thing we can do together to make things better is:

Do you need advice? **If so, what advice are you looking for?**

KID SITUATION________________________________

These words can sometimes be a bridge to opening up, making it easier to share feelings in a way that resonates. Circle a word, or words, that match your feelings currently. This helps who you're communicating with, know where you're coming from in your heart and mind.

Feel-Good Emotions:		**Hard-to-Discuss Feelings:**	
Grateful	Excited	Vulnerable	Resentful
Loved	Confident	Isolated	Unheard
Happy	Supported	Anxious	Trapped
Peaceful	Encouraged	Overwhelmed	Hopeless
Proud	Secure	Insecure	Lonely
Joyful	Hopeful	Misunderstood	Defeated
Appreciated	Inspired	Conflicted	Ashamed

Describe how you're feeling right now. Are you sad, angry, frustrated, worried, or something else? Write about why you're feeling this way.

I'm feeling:

____

____

____

____

____

____

____

____

____

What could my adult do to help you feel better?
Maybe you need space, a hug, or just for them to listen.

What I need from you is:

What things can you both do to solve the problem?
Maybe spend time talking, set up a new rule, or agree on a plan.

One thing we can do together to make things better is:

Do you need advice? **If so, what advice are you looking for?**

KID REFLECTION SITUATION________________________________

- How I feel about our progress so far is:

____
____
____
____
____
____

- One thing I've learned about my adult/adults is:

____
____
____
____
____
____

- One thing I still need help with is:

____
____
____
____
____
____

SITUATION____

ADULT REFLECTION

- How I feel about our progress so far is:

____
____
____
____
____
____

- One thing I've learned about my kid is:

____
____
____
____
____
____

- One thing we can continue to work on is:

____
____
____
____
____
____

ADULT SITUATION_______________________________

These words can sometimes be a bridge to opening up, making it easier to share feelings in a way that resonates. Circle a word, or words, that match your feelings currently. This helps who you're communicating with, know where you're coming from in your heart and mind.

Feel-Good Emotions:		Hard-to-Discuss Feelings:	
Grateful	Excited	Vulnerable	Resentful
Loved	Confident	Isolated	Unheard
Happy	Supported	Anxious	Trapped
Peaceful	Encouraged	Overwhelmed	Hopeless
Proud	Secure	Insecure	Lonely
Joyful	Hopeful	Misunderstood	Defeated
Appreciated	Inspired	Conflicted	Ashamed

Describe how you're feeling right now. Are you sad, angry, frustrated, worried, or something else? Write about why you're feeling this way.

I'm feeling:

What could my kid do to help?
Maybe you need them to listen, follow a rule, or talk calmly.

What I need from you is:

What things can you both do to solve the problem?
Maybe spend time talking, set up a new rule, or agree on a plan.

One thing we can do together to make things better is:

Do you need advice? **If so, what advice are you looking for?**

KID SITUATION____

These words can sometimes be a bridge to opening up, making it easier to share feelings in a way that resonates. Circle a word, or words, that match your feelings currently. This helps who you're communicating with, know where you're coming from in your heart and mind.

Feel-Good Emotions:		**Hard-to-Discuss Feelings:**	
Grateful	Excited	Vulnerable	Resentful
Loved	Confident	Isolated	Unheard
Happy	Supported	Anxious	Trapped
Peaceful	Encouraged	Overwhelmed	Hopeless
Proud	Secure	Insecure	Lonely
Joyful	Hopeful	Misunderstood	Defeated
Appreciated	Inspired	Conflicted	Ashamed

Describe how you're feeling right now. Are you sad, angry, frustrated, worried, or something else? Write about why you're feeling this way.

I'm feeling:

____

____

____

____

____

____

____

____

____

What could my adult do to help you feel better?
Maybe you need space, a hug, or just for them to listen.

What I need from you is:

____

____

____

____

____

____

____

____

What things can you both do to solve the problem?
Maybe spend time talking, set up a new rule, or agree on a plan.

One thing we can do together to make things better is:

____

Do you need advice? **If so, what advice are you looking for?**

____

____

____

____

____

____

____

____

KID REFLECTION SITUATION______________________________

- How I feel about our progress so far is:

____
____
____
____
____
____

- One thing I've learned about my adult/adults is:

____
____
____
____
____
____

- One thing I still need help with is:

____
____
____
____
____
____

SITUATION____

ADULT REFLECTION

- How I feel about our progress so far is:

- One thing I've learned about my kid is:

- One thing we can continue to work on is:

ADULT SITUATION____

These words can sometimes be a bridge to opening up, making it easier to share feelings in a way that resonates. Circle a word, or words, that match your feelings currently. This helps who you're communicating with, know where you're coming from in your heart and mind.

Feel-Good Emotions:		**Hard-to-Discuss Feelings:**	
Grateful	Excited	Vulnerable	Resentful
Loved	Confident	Isolated	Unheard
Happy	Supported	Anxious	Trapped
Peaceful	Encouraged	Overwhelmed	Hopeless
Proud	Secure	Insecure	Lonely
Joyful	Hopeful	Misunderstood	Defeated
Appreciated	Inspired	Conflicted	Ashamed

Describe how you're feeling right now. Are you sad, angry, frustrated, worried, or something else? Write about why you're feeling this way.

I'm feeling:

____

____

____

____

____

____

____

____

____

What could my kid do to help?
Maybe you need them to listen, follow a rule, or talk calmly.

What I need from you is:

What things can you both do to solve the problem?
Maybe spend time talking, set up a new rule, or agree on a plan.

One thing we can do together to make things better is:

Do you need advice? **If so, what advice are you looking for?**

KID

SITUATION ____________________

These words can sometimes be a bridge to opening up, making it easier to share feelings in a way that resonates. Circle a word, or words, that match your feelings currently. This helps who you're communicating with, know where you're coming from in your heart and mind.

Feel-Good Emotions:		**Hard-to-Discuss Feelings:**	
Grateful	Excited	Vulnerable	Resentful
Loved	Confident	Isolated	Unheard
Happy	Supported	Anxious	Trapped
Peaceful	Encouraged	Overwhelmed	Hopeless
Proud	Secure	Insecure	Lonely
Joyful	Hopeful	Misunderstood	Defeated
Appreciated	Inspired	Conflicted	Ashamed

Describe how you're feeling right now. Are you sad, angry, frustrated, worried, or something else? Write about why you're feeling this way.

I'm feeling:

____

____

____

____

____

____

____

____

____

What could my adult do to help you feel better?
Maybe you need space, a hug, or just for them to listen.

What I need from you is:

____

____

____

____

____

____

____

____

What things can you both do to solve the problem?
Maybe spend time talking, set up a new rule, or agree on a plan.

One thing we can do together to make things better is:

____

Do you need advice? **If so, what advice are you looking for?**

____

____

____

____

____

____

____

____

KID REFLECTION SITUATION________________________________

- How I feel about our progress so far is:

____

____

____

____

____

____

- One thing I've learned about my adult/adults is:

____

____

____

____

____

____

- One thing I still need help with is:

____

____

____

____

____

____

SITUATION___________________________________

ADULT REFLECTION

- How I feel about our progress so far is:

____

____

____

____

____

____

- One thing I've learned about my kid is:

____

____

____

____

____

____

- One thing we can continue to work on is:

____

____

____

____

____

____

ADULT SITUATION____

These words can sometimes be a bridge to opening up, making it easier to share feelings in a way that resonates. Circle a word, or words, that match your feelings currently. This helps who you're communicating with, know where you're coming from in your heart and mind.

Feel-Good Emotions:		**Hard-to-Discuss Feelings:**	
Grateful	Excited	Vulnerable	Resentful
Loved	Confident	Isolated	Unheard
Happy	Supported	Anxious	Trapped
Peaceful	Encouraged	Overwhelmed	Hopeless
Proud	Secure	Insecure	Lonely
Joyful	Hopeful	Misunderstood	Defeated
Appreciated	Inspired	Conflicted	Ashamed

Describe how you're feeling right now. Are you sad, angry, frustrated, worried, or something else? Write about why you're feeling this way.

I'm feeling:

____

____

____

____

____

____

____

____

____

What could my kid do to help?
Maybe you need them to listen, follow a rule, or talk calmly.

What I need from you is:

____

____

____

____

____

____

____

____

____

What things can you both do to solve the problem?
Maybe spend time talking, set up a new rule, or agree on a plan.

One thing we can do together to make things better is:

____

Do you need advice? **If so, what advice are you looking for?**

____

____

____

____

____

____

____

KID SITUATION____

These words can sometimes be a bridge to opening up, making it easier to share feelings in a way that resonates. Circle a word, or words, that match your feelings currently. This helps who you're communicating with, know where you're coming from in your heart and mind.

Feel-Good Emotions:		**Hard-to-Discuss Feelings:**	
Grateful	Excited	Vulnerable	Resentful
Loved	Confident	Isolated	Unheard
Happy	Supported	Anxious	Trapped
Peaceful	Encouraged	Overwhelmed	Hopeless
Proud	Secure	Insecure	Lonely
Joyful	Hopeful	Misunderstood	Defeated
Appreciated	Inspired	Conflicted	Ashamed

Describe how you're feeling right now. Are you sad, angry, frustrated, worried, or something else? Write about why you're feeling this way.

I'm feeling:

____

____

____

____

____

____

____

____

____

What could my adult do to help you feel better?
Maybe you need space, a hug, or just for them to listen.

What I need from you is:

What things can you both do to solve the problem?
Maybe spend time talking, set up a new rule, or agree on a plan.

One thing we can do together to make things better is:

Do you need advice? **If so, what advice are you looking for?**

KID REFLECTION

SITUATION____

- How I feel about our progress so far is:

____

____

____

____

____

____

- One thing I've learned about my adult/adults is:

____

____

____

____

____

____

- One thing I still need help with is:

____

____

____

____

____

____

SITUATION____

ADULT REFLECTION

- How I feel about our progress so far is:

____

____

____

____

____

____

- One thing I've learned about my kid is:

____

____

____

____

____

____

- One thing we can continue to work on is:

____

____

____

____

____

____

ADULT SITUATION________________________________

These words can sometimes be a bridge to opening up, making it easier to share feelings in a way that resonates. Circle a word, or words, that match your feelings currently. This helps who you're communicating with, know where you're coming from in your heart and mind.

Feel-Good Emotions:		**Hard-to-Discuss Feelings:**	
Grateful	Excited	Vulnerable	Resentful
Loved	Confident	Isolated	Unheard
Happy	Supported	Anxious	Trapped
Peaceful	Encouraged	Overwhelmed	Hopeless
Proud	Secure	Insecure	Lonely
Joyful	Hopeful	Misunderstood	Defeated
Appreciated	Inspired	Conflicted	Ashamed

Describe how you're feeling right now. Are you sad, angry, frustrated, worried, or something else? Write about why you're feeling this way.

I'm feeling:

____

____

____

____

____

____

____

____

____

What could my kid do to help?
Maybe you need them to listen, follow a rule, or talk calmly.

What I need from you is:

What things can you both do to solve the problem?
Maybe spend time talking, set up a new rule, or agree on a plan.

One thing we can do together to make things better is:

Do you need advice? **If so, what advice are you looking for?**

KID SITUATION________________________________

These words can sometimes be a bridge to opening up, making it easier to share feelings in a way that resonates. Circle a word, or words, that match your feelings currently. This helps who you're communicating with, know where you're coming from in your heart and mind.

Feel-Good Emotions:		**Hard-to-Discuss Feelings:**	
Grateful	Excited	Vulnerable	Resentful
Loved	Confident	Isolated	Unheard
Happy	Supported	Anxious	Trapped
Peaceful	Encouraged	Overwhelmed	Hopeless
Proud	Secure	Insecure	Lonely
Joyful	Hopeful	Misunderstood	Defeated
Appreciated	Inspired	Conflicted	Ashamed

Describe how you're feeling right now. Are you sad, angry, frustrated, worried, or something else? Write about why you're feeling this way.

I'm feeling:

____

____

____

____

____

____

____

____

____

What could my adult do to help you feel better?
Maybe you need space, a hug, or just for them to listen.

What I need from you is:

What things can you both do to solve the problem?
Maybe spend time talking, set up a new rule, or agree on a plan.

One thing we can do together to make things better is:

Do you need advice? **If so, what advice are you looking for?**

KID REFLECTION SITUATION ______________________________

- How I feel about our progress so far is:

____

____

____

____

____

____

- One thing I've learned about my adult/adults is:

____

____

____

____

____

____

- One thing I still need help with is:

____

____

____

____

____

____

SITUATION____

ADULT REFLECTION

- How I feel about our progress so far is:

____

____

____

____

____

____

- One thing I've learned about my kid is:

____

____

____

____

____

____

- One thing we can continue to work on is:

____

____

____

____

____

____

ADULT SITUATION________________________________

These words can sometimes be a bridge to opening up, making it easier to share feelings in a way that resonates. Circle a word, or words, that match your feelings currently. This helps who you're communicating with, know where you're coming from in your heart and mind.

Feel-Good Emotions:		**Hard-to-Discuss Feelings:**	
Grateful	Excited	Vulnerable	Resentful
Loved	Confident	Isolated	Unheard
Happy	Supported	Anxious	Trapped
Peaceful	Encouraged	Overwhelmed	Hopeless
Proud	Secure	Insecure	Lonely
Joyful	Hopeful	Misunderstood	Defeated
Appreciated	Inspired	Conflicted	Ashamed

Describe how you're feeling right now. Are you sad, angry, frustrated, worried, or something else? Write about why you're feeling this way.

I'm feeling:

____

____

____

____

____

____

____

____

____

What could my kid do to help?
Maybe you need them to listen, follow a rule, or talk calmly.

What I need from you is:

What things can you both do to solve the problem?
Maybe spend time talking, set up a new rule, or agree on a plan.

One thing we can do together to make things better is:

Do you need advice? **If so, what advice are you looking for?**

KID SITUATION________________________________

These words can sometimes be a bridge to opening up, making it easier to share feelings in a way that resonates. Circle a word, or words, that match your feelings currently. This helps who you're communicating with, know where you're coming from in your heart and mind.

Feel-Good Emotions:		**Hard-to-Discuss Feelings:**	
Grateful	Excited	Vulnerable	Resentful
Loved	Confident	Isolated	Unheard
Happy	Supported	Anxious	Trapped
Peaceful	Encouraged	Overwhelmed	Hopeless
Proud	Secure	Insecure	Lonely
Joyful	Hopeful	Misunderstood	Defeated
Appreciated	Inspired	Conflicted	Ashamed

Describe how you're feeling right now. Are you sad, angry, frustrated, worried, or something else? Write about why you're feeling this way.

I'm feeling:

____

____

____

____

____

____

____

____

____

What could my adult do to help you feel better?
Maybe you need space, a hug, or just for them to listen.

What I need from you is:

____

____

____

____

____

____

____

____

What things can you both do to solve the problem?
Maybe spend time talking, set up a new rule, or agree on a plan.

One thing we can do together to make things better is:

____

Do you need advice? **If so, what advice are you looking for?**

____

____

____

____

____

____

____

____

KID REFLECTION

SITUATION ____

- How I feel about our progress so far is:

____

____

____

____

____

____

- One thing I've learned about my adult/adults is:

____

____

____

____

____

____

- One thing I still need help with is:

____

____

____

____

____

____

SITUATION____

ADULT REFLECTION

- How I feel about our progress so far is:

____

____

____

____

____

____

- One thing I've learned about my kid is:

____

____

____

____

____

____

- One thing we can continue to work on is:

____

____

____

____

____

____

ADULT SITUATION______________________________________

These words can sometimes be a bridge to opening up, making it easier to share feelings in a way that resonates. Circle a word, or words, that match your feelings currently. This helps who you're communicating with, know where you're coming from in your heart and mind.

Feel-Good Emotions:		**Hard-to-Discuss Feelings:**	
Grateful	Excited	Vulnerable	Resentful
Loved	Confident	Isolated	Unheard
Happy	Supported	Anxious	Trapped
Peaceful	Encouraged	Overwhelmed	Hopeless
Proud	Secure	Insecure	Lonely
Joyful	Hopeful	Misunderstood	Defeated
Appreciated	Inspired	Conflicted	Ashamed

Describe how you're feeling right now. Are you sad, angry, frustrated, worried, or something else? Write about why you're feeling this way.

I'm feeling:

____

____

____

____

____

____

____

____

____

What could my kid do to help?
Maybe you need them to listen, follow a rule, or talk calmly.

What I need from you is:

____

____

____

____

____

____

____

____

____

What things can you both do to solve the problem?
Maybe spend time talking, set up a new rule, or agree on a plan.

One thing we can do together to make things better is:

____

Do you need advice? **If so, what advice are you looking for?**

____

____

____

____

____

____

____

KID SITUATION ______________________________

These words can sometimes be a bridge to opening up, making it easier to share feelings in a way that resonates. Circle a word, or words, that match your feelings currently. This helps who you're communicating with, know where you're coming from in your heart and mind.

Feel-Good Emotions:		**Hard-to-Discuss Feelings:**	
Grateful	Excited	Vulnerable	Resentful
Loved	Confident	Isolated	Unheard
Happy	Supported	Anxious	Trapped
Peaceful	Encouraged	Overwhelmed	Hopeless
Proud	Secure	Insecure	Lonely
Joyful	Hopeful	Misunderstood	Defeated
Appreciated	Inspired	Conflicted	Ashamed

Describe how you're feeling right now. Are you sad, angry, frustrated, worried, or something else? Write about why you're feeling this way.

I'm feeling:

____

____

____

____

____

____

____

____

____

What could my adult do to help you feel better?
Maybe you need space, a hug, or just for them to listen.

What I need from you is:

What things can you both do to solve the problem?
Maybe spend time talking, set up a new rule, or agree on a plan.

One thing we can do together to make things better is:

Do you need advice? **If so, what advice are you looking for?**

KID REFLECTION

SITUATION______________________________

- How I feel about our progress so far is:

____
____
____
____
____
____

- One thing I've learned about my adult/adults is:

____
____
____
____
____
____

- One thing I still need help with is:

____
____
____
____
____
____

SITUATION______________________________________

ADULT REFLECTION

- How I feel about our progress so far is:

____

____

____

____

____

____

- One thing I've learned about my kid is:

____

____

____

____

____

____

- One thing we can continue to work on is:

____

____

____

____

____

____

ADULT SITUATION________________________________

These words can sometimes be a bridge to opening up, making it easier to share feelings in a way that resonates. Circle a word, or words, that match your feelings currently. This helps who you're communicating with, know where you're coming from in your heart and mind.

Feel-Good Emotions:		**Hard-to-Discuss Feelings:**	
Grateful	Excited	Vulnerable	Resentful
Loved	Confident	Isolated	Unheard
Happy	Supported	Anxious	Trapped
Peaceful	Encouraged	Overwhelmed	Hopeless
Proud	Secure	Insecure	Lonely
Joyful	Hopeful	Misunderstood	Defeated
Appreciated	Inspired	Conflicted	Ashamed

Describe how you're feeling right now. Are you sad, angry, frustrated, worried, or something else? Write about why you're feeling this way.

I'm feeling:

____

____

____

____

____

____

____

____

____

What could my kid do to help?
Maybe you need them to listen, follow a rule, or talk calmly.

What I need from you is:

What things can you both do to solve the problem?
Maybe spend time talking, set up a new rule, or agree on a plan.

One thing we can do together to make things better is:

Do you need advice? **If so, what advice are you looking for?**

KID SITUATION____

These words can sometimes be a bridge to opening up, making it easier to share feelings in a way that resonates. Circle a word, or words, that match your feelings currently. This helps who you're communicating with, know where you're coming from in your heart and mind.

Feel-Good Emotions:		**Hard-to-Discuss Feelings:**	
Grateful	Excited	Vulnerable	Resentful
Loved	Confident	Isolated	Unheard
Happy	Supported	Anxious	Trapped
Peaceful	Encouraged	Overwhelmed	Hopeless
Proud	Secure	Insecure	Lonely
Joyful	Hopeful	Misunderstood	Defeated
Appreciated	Inspired	Conflicted	Ashamed

Describe how you're feeling right now. Are you sad, angry, frustrated, worried, or something else? Write about why you're feeling this way.

I'm feeling:

____

____

____

____

____

____

____

____

____

What could my adult do to help you feel better?
Maybe you need space, a hug, or just for them to listen.

What I need from you is:

What things can you both do to solve the problem?
Maybe spend time talking, set up a new rule, or agree on a plan.

One thing we can do together to make things better is:

Do you need advice? **If so, what advice are you looking for?**

KID REFLECTION SITUATION ______________________

- How I feel about our progress so far is:

____
____
____
____
____
____

- One thing I've learned about my adult/adults is:

____
____
____
____
____
____

- One thing I still need help with is:

____
____
____
____
____
____

SITUATION________________________________

ADULT REFLECTION

- How I feel about our progress so far is:

____

____

____

____

____

____

- One thing I've learned about my kid is:

____

____

____

____

____

____

- One thing we can continue to work on is:

____

____

____

____

____

____

ADULT SITUATION ______________________________

These words can sometimes be a bridge to opening up, making it easier to share feelings in a way that resonates. Circle a word, or words, that match your feelings currently. This helps who you're communicating with, know where you're coming from in your heart and mind.

Feel-Good Emotions:		**Hard-to-Discuss Feelings:**	
Grateful	Excited	Vulnerable	Resentful
Loved	Confident	Isolated	Unheard
Happy	Supported	Anxious	Trapped
Peaceful	Encouraged	Overwhelmed	Hopeless
Proud	Secure	Insecure	Lonely
Joyful	Hopeful	Misunderstood	Defeated
Appreciated	Inspired	Conflicted	Ashamed

Describe how you're feeling right now. Are you sad, angry, frustrated, worried, or something else? Write about why you're feeling this way.

I'm feeling:

____

____

____

____

____

____

____

____

____

What could my kid do to help?
Maybe you need them to listen, follow a rule, or talk calmly.

What I need from you is:

What things can you both do to solve the problem?
Maybe spend time talking, set up a new rule, or agree on a plan.

One thing we can do together to make things better is:

Do you need advice? **If so, what advice are you looking for?**

KID SITUATION____

These words can sometimes be a bridge to opening up, making it easier to share feelings in a way that resonates. Circle a word, or words, that match your feelings currently. This helps who you're communicating with, know where you're coming from in your heart and mind.

Feel-Good Emotions:		**Hard-to-Discuss Feelings:**	
Grateful	Excited	Vulnerable	Resentful
Loved	Confident	Isolated	Unheard
Happy	Supported	Anxious	Trapped
Peaceful	Encouraged	Overwhelmed	Hopeless
Proud	Secure	Insecure	Lonely
Joyful	Hopeful	Misunderstood	Defeated
Appreciated	Inspired	Conflicted	Ashamed

Describe how you're feeling right now. Are you sad, angry, frustrated, worried, or something else? Write about why you're feeling this way.

I'm feeling:

____

____

____

____

____

____

____

____

____

What could my adult do to help you feel better?
Maybe you need space, a hug, or just for them to listen.

What I need from you is:

What things can you both do to solve the problem?
Maybe spend time talking, set up a new rule, or agree on a plan.

One thing we can do together to make things better is:

Do you need advice? **If so, what advice are you looking for?**

KID REFLECTION SITUATION______________________________

- How I feel about our progress so far is:

____
____
____
____
____
____

- One thing I've learned about my adult/adults is:

____
____
____
____
____
____

- One thing I still need help with is:

____
____
____
____
____
____

ADULT REFLECTION

SITUATION____

- How I feel about our progress so far is:

____

____

____

____

____

____

- One thing I've learned about my kid is:

____

____

____

____

____

____

- One thing we can continue to work on is:

____

____

____

____

____

____

ADULT SITUATION____

These words can sometimes be a bridge to opening up, making it easier to share feelings in a way that resonates. Circle a word, or words, that match your feelings currently. This helps who you're communicating with, know where you're coming from in your heart and mind.

Feel-Good Emotions:		Hard-to-Discuss Feelings:	
Grateful	Excited	Vulnerable	Resentful
Loved	Confident	Isolated	Unheard
Happy	Supported	Anxious	Trapped
Peaceful	Encouraged	Overwhelmed	Hopeless
Proud	Secure	Insecure	Lonely
Joyful	Hopeful	Misunderstood	Defeated
Appreciated	Inspired	Conflicted	Ashamed

Describe how you're feeling right now. Are you sad, angry, frustrated, worried, or something else? Write about why you're feeling this way.

I'm feeling:

____

____

____

____

____

____

____

____

____

What could my kid do to help?
Maybe you need them to listen, follow a rule, or talk calmly.

What I need from you is:

What things can you both do to solve the problem?
Maybe spend time talking, set up a new rule, or agree on a plan.

One thing we can do together to make things better is:

Do you need advice? **If so, what advice are you looking for?**

KID SITUATION____

These words can sometimes be a bridge to opening up, making it easier to share feelings in a way that resonates. Circle a word, or words, that match your feelings currently. This helps who you're communicating with, know where you're coming from in your heart and mind.

Feel-Good Emotions:		**Hard-to-Discuss Feelings:**	
Grateful	Excited	Vulnerable	Resentful
Loved	Confident	Isolated	Unheard
Happy	Supported	Anxious	Trapped
Peaceful	Encouraged	Overwhelmed	Hopeless
Proud	Secure	Insecure	Lonely
Joyful	Hopeful	Misunderstood	Defeated
Appreciated	Inspired	Conflicted	Ashamed

Describe how you're feeling right now. Are you sad, angry, frustrated, worried, or something else? Write about why you're feeling this way.

I'm feeling:

____

____

____

____

____

____

____

____

____

What could my adult do to help you feel better?
Maybe you need space, a hug, or just for them to listen.

What I need from you is:

____

____

____

____

____

____

____

____

What things can you both do to solve the problem?
Maybe spend time talking, set up a new rule, or agree on a plan.

One thing we can do together to make things better is:

____

Do you need advice? **If so, what advice are you looking for?**

____

____

____

____

____

____

____

____

KID REFLECTION SITUATION ______________________

- How I feel about our progress so far is:

____
____
____
____
____
____

- One thing I've learned about my adult/adults is:

____
____
____
____
____
____

- One thing I still need help with is:

____
____
____
____
____
____

SITUATION____

ADULT REFLECTION

- How I feel about our progress so far is:

____

____

____

____

____

____

- One thing I've learned about my kid is:

____

____

____

____

____

____

- One thing we can continue to work on is:

____

____

____

____

____

____

ADULT SITUATION____

These words can sometimes be a bridge to opening up, making it easier to share feelings in a way that resonates. Circle a word, or words, that match your feelings currently. This helps who you're communicating with, know where you're coming from in your heart and mind.

Feel-Good Emotions:		**Hard-to-Discuss Feelings:**	
Grateful	Excited	Vulnerable	Resentful
Loved	Confident	Isolated	Unheard
Happy	Supported	Anxious	Trapped
Peaceful	Encouraged	Overwhelmed	Hopeless
Proud	Secure	Insecure	Lonely
Joyful	Hopeful	Misunderstood	Defeated
Appreciated	Inspired	Conflicted	Ashamed

Describe how you're feeling right now. Are you sad, angry, frustrated, worried, or something else? Write about why you're feeling this way.

I'm feeling:

____

____

____

____

____

____

____

____

____

What could my kid do to help?
Maybe you need them to listen, follow a rule, or talk calmly.

What I need from you is:

What things can you both do to solve the problem?
Maybe spend time talking, set up a new rule, or agree on a plan.

One thing we can do together to make things better is:

Do you need advice? **If so, what advice are you looking for?**

KID SITUATION________________________________

These words can sometimes be a bridge to opening up, making it easier to share feelings in a way that resonates. Circle a word, or words, that match your feelings currently. This helps who you're communicating with, know where you're coming from in your heart and mind.

Feel-Good Emotions:		**Hard-to-Discuss Feelings:**	
Grateful	Excited	Vulnerable	Resentful
Loved	Confident	Isolated	Unheard
Happy	Supported	Anxious	Trapped
Peaceful	Encouraged	Overwhelmed	Hopeless
Proud	Secure	Insecure	Lonely
Joyful	Hopeful	Misunderstood	Defeated
Appreciated	Inspired	Conflicted	Ashamed

Describe how you're feeling right now. Are you sad, angry, frustrated, worried, or something else? Write about why you're feeling this way.

I'm feeling:

____

____

____

____

____

____

____

____

____

What could my adult do to help you feel better?
Maybe you need space, a hug, or just for them to listen.

What I need from you is:

What things can you both do to solve the problem?
Maybe spend time talking, set up a new rule, or agree on a plan.

One thing we can do together to make things better is:

Do you need advice? **If so, what advice are you looking for?**

KID REFLECTION

SITUATION __________________________________

- How I feel about our progress so far is:

- One thing I've learned about my adult/adults is:

- One thing I still need help with is:

SITUATION____

ADULT REFLECTION

- How I feel about our progress so far is:

____

____

____

____

____

____

- One thing I've learned about my kid is:

____

____

____

____

____

____

- One thing we can continue to work on is:

____

____

____

____

____

____

ADULT SITUATION________________________________

These words can sometimes be a bridge to opening up, making it easier to share feelings in a way that resonates. Circle a word, or words, that match your feelings currently. This helps who you're communicating with, know where you're coming from in your heart and mind.

Feel-Good Emotions:		**Hard-to-Discuss Feelings:**	
Grateful	Excited	Vulnerable	Resentful
Loved	Confident	Isolated	Unheard
Happy	Supported	Anxious	Trapped
Peaceful	Encouraged	Overwhelmed	Hopeless
Proud	Secure	Insecure	Lonely
Joyful	Hopeful	Misunderstood	Defeated
Appreciated	Inspired	Conflicted	Ashamed

Describe how you're feeling right now. Are you sad, angry, frustrated, worried, or something else? Write about why you're feeling this way.

I'm feeling:

____

____

____

____

____

____

____

____

____

What could my kid do to help?
Maybe you need them to listen, follow a rule, or talk calmly.

What I need from you is:

What things can you both do to solve the problem?
Maybe spend time talking, set up a new rule, or agree on a plan.

One thing we can do together to make things better is:

Do you need advice? **If so, what advice are you looking for?**

KID SITUATION________________________________

These words can sometimes be a bridge to opening up, making it easier to share feelings in a way that resonates. Circle a word, or words, that match your feelings currently. This helps who you're communicating with, know where you're coming from in your heart and mind.

Feel-Good Emotions:		**Hard-to-Discuss Feelings:**	
Grateful	Excited	Vulnerable	Resentful
Loved	Confident	Isolated	Unheard
Happy	Supported	Anxious	Trapped
Peaceful	Encouraged	Overwhelmed	Hopeless
Proud	Secure	Insecure	Lonely
Joyful	Hopeful	Misunderstood	Defeated
Appreciated	Inspired	Conflicted	Ashamed

Describe how you're feeling right now. Are you sad, angry, frustrated, worried, or something else? Write about why you're feeling this way.

I'm feeling:

____

____

____

____

____

____

____

____

____

What could my adult do to help you feel better?
Maybe you need space, a hug, or just for them to listen.

What I need from you is:

____

____

____

____

____

____

____

____

What things can you both do to solve the problem?
Maybe spend time talking, set up a new rule, or agree on a plan.

One thing we can do together to make things better is:

____

Do you need advice? **If so, what advice are you looking for?**

____

____

____

____

____

____

____

____

KID REFLECTION SITUATION ______________________________

- How I feel about our progress so far is:

____
____
____
____
____
____

- One thing I've learned about my adult/adults is:

____
____
____
____
____
____

- One thing I still need help with is:

____
____
____
____
____
____

SITUATION____

ADULT REFLECTION

- How I feel about our progress so far is:

____

____

____

____

____

____

- One thing I've learned about my kid is:

____

____

____

____

____

____

- One thing we can continue to work on is:

____

____

____

____

____

____

ADULT SITUATION________________________________

These words can sometimes be a bridge to opening up, making it easier to share feelings in a way that resonates. Circle a word, or words, that match your feelings currently. This helps who you're communicating with, know where you're coming from in your heart and mind.

Feel-Good Emotions:		**Hard-to-Discuss Feelings:**	
Grateful	Excited	Vulnerable	Resentful
Loved	Confident	Isolated	Unheard
Happy	Supported	Anxious	Trapped
Peaceful	Encouraged	Overwhelmed	Hopeless
Proud	Secure	Insecure	Lonely
Joyful	Hopeful	Misunderstood	Defeated
Appreciated	Inspired	Conflicted	Ashamed

Describe how you're feeling right now. Are you sad, angry, frustrated, worried, or something else? Write about why you're feeling this way.

I'm feeling:

____

____

____

____

____

____

____

____

____

What could my kid do to help?
Maybe you need them to listen, follow a rule, or talk calmly.

What I need from you is:

What things can you both do to solve the problem?
Maybe spend time talking, set up a new rule, or agree on a plan.

One thing we can do together to make things better is:

Do you need advice? **If so, what advice are you looking for?**

KID SITUATION____

These words can sometimes be a bridge to opening up, making it easier to share feelings in a way that resonates. Circle a word, or words, that match your feelings currently. This helps who you're communicating with, know where you're coming from in your heart and mind.

Feel-Good Emotions:		**Hard-to-Discuss Feelings:**	
Grateful	Excited	Vulnerable	Resentful
Loved	Confident	Isolated	Unheard
Happy	Supported	Anxious	Trapped
Peaceful	Encouraged	Overwhelmed	Hopeless
Proud	Secure	Insecure	Lonely
Joyful	Hopeful	Misunderstood	Defeated
Appreciated	Inspired	Conflicted	Ashamed

Describe how you're feeling right now. Are you sad, angry, frustrated, worried, or something else? Write about why you're feeling this way.

I'm feeling:

____

____

____

____

____

____

____

____

____

What could my adult do to help you feel better?
Maybe you need space, a hug, or just for them to listen.

What I need from you is:

____

____

____

____

____

____

____

____

What things can you both do to solve the problem?
Maybe spend time talking, set up a new rule, or agree on a plan.

One thing we can do together to make things better is:

____

Do you need advice? **If so, what advice are you looking for?**

____

____

____

____

____

____

____

____

KID REFLECTION

SITUATION ______________________________

- How I feel about our progress so far is:

____

____

____

____

____

____

- One thing I've learned about my adult/adults is:

____

____

____

____

____

____

- One thing I still need help with is:

____

____

____

____

____

____

SITUATION____

ADULT REFLECTION

- How I feel about our progress so far is:

____

____

____

____

____

____

- One thing I've learned about my kid is:

____

____

____

____

____

____

- One thing we can continue to work on is:

____

____

____

____

____

____

ADULT SITUATION________________________________

These words can sometimes be a bridge to opening up, making it easier to share feelings in a way that resonates. Circle a word, or words, that match your feelings currently. This helps who you're communicating with, know where you're coming from in your heart and mind.

Feel-Good Emotions:		Hard-to-Discuss Feelings:	
Grateful	Excited	Vulnerable	Resentful
Loved	Confident	Isolated	Unheard
Happy	Supported	Anxious	Trapped
Peaceful	Encouraged	Overwhelmed	Hopeless
Proud	Secure	Insecure	Lonely
Joyful	Hopeful	Misunderstood	Defeated
Appreciated	Inspired	Conflicted	Ashamed

Describe how you're feeling right now. Are you sad, angry, frustrated, worried, or something else? Write about why you're feeling this way.

I'm feeling:

____

____

____

____

____

____

____

____

____

What could my kid do to help?
Maybe you need them to listen, follow a rule, or talk calmly.

What I need from you is:

____

____

____

____

____

____

____

____

____

What things can you both do to solve the problem?
Maybe spend time talking, set up a new rule, or agree on a plan.

One thing we can do together to make things better is:

____

Do you need advice? **If so, what advice are you looking for?**

____

____

____

____

____

____

____

KID SITUATION______________________________________

These words can sometimes be a bridge to opening up, making it easier to share feelings in a way that resonates. Circle a word, or words, that match your feelings currently. This helps who you're communicating with, know where you're coming from in your heart and mind.

Feel-Good Emotions:		**Hard-to-Discuss Feelings:**	
Grateful	Excited	Vulnerable	Resentful
Loved	Confident	Isolated	Unheard
Happy	Supported	Anxious	Trapped
Peaceful	Encouraged	Overwhelmed	Hopeless
Proud	Secure	Insecure	Lonely
Joyful	Hopeful	Misunderstood	Defeated
Appreciated	Inspired	Conflicted	Ashamed

Describe how you're feeling right now. Are you sad, angry, frustrated, worried, or something else? Write about why you're feeling this way.

I'm feeling:

____

____

____

____

____

____

____

____

____

What could my adult do to help you feel better?
Maybe you need space, a hug, or just for them to listen.

What I need from you is:

____

____

____

____

____

____

____

____

What things can you both do to solve the problem?
Maybe spend time talking, set up a new rule, or agree on a plan.

One thing we can do together to make things better is:

____

Do you need advice? **If so, what advice are you looking for?**

____

____

____

____

____

____

____

____

KID REFLECTION SITUATION ____________________________________

- How I feel about our progress so far is:

____

____

____

____

____

____

- One thing I've learned about my adult/adults is:

____

____

____

____

____

____

- One thing I still need help with is:

____

____

____

____

____

____

SITUATION____

ADULT REFLECTION

- How I feel about our progress so far is:

____

____

____

____

____

____

- One thing I've learned about my kid is:

____

____

____

____

____

____

- One thing we can continue to work on is:

____

____

____

____

____

____

ADULT SITUATION____

These words can sometimes be a bridge to opening up, making it easier to share feelings in a way that resonates. Circle a word, or words, that match your feelings currently. This helps who you're communicating with, know where you're coming from in your heart and mind.

Feel-Good Emotions:		**Hard-to-Discuss Feelings:**	
Grateful	Excited	Vulnerable	Resentful
Loved	Confident	Isolated	Unheard
Happy	Supported	Anxious	Trapped
Peaceful	Encouraged	Overwhelmed	Hopeless
Proud	Secure	Insecure	Lonely
Joyful	Hopeful	Misunderstood	Defeated
Appreciated	Inspired	Conflicted	Ashamed

Describe how you're feeling right now. Are you sad, angry, frustrated, worried, or something else? Write about why you're feeling this way.

I'm feeling:

____

____

____

____

____

____

____

____

____

What could my kid do to help?
Maybe you need them to listen, follow a rule, or talk calmly.

What I need from you is:

What things can you both do to solve the problem?
Maybe spend time talking, set up a new rule, or agree on a plan.

One thing we can do together to make things better is:

Do you need advice? **If so, what advice are you looking for?**

KID SITUATION______________________________

These words can sometimes be a bridge to opening up, making it easier to share feelings in a way that resonates. Circle a word, or words, that match your feelings currently. This helps who you're communicating with, know where you're coming from in your heart and mind.

Feel-Good Emotions:		**Hard-to-Discuss Feelings:**	
Grateful	Excited	Vulnerable	Resentful
Loved	Confident	Isolated	Unheard
Happy	Supported	Anxious	Trapped
Peaceful	Encouraged	Overwhelmed	Hopeless
Proud	Secure	Insecure	Lonely
Joyful	Hopeful	Misunderstood	Defeated
Appreciated	Inspired	Conflicted	Ashamed

Describe how you're feeling right now. Are you sad, angry, frustrated, worried, or something else? Write about why you're feeling this way.

I'm feeling:

____

____

____

____

____

____

____

____

____

What could my adult do to help you feel better?
Maybe you need space, a hug, or just for them to listen.

What I need from you is:

What things can you both do to solve the problem?
Maybe spend time talking, set up a new rule, or agree on a plan.

One thing we can do together to make things better is:

Do you need advice? **If so, what advice are you looking for?**

KID REFLECTION

SITUATION______________________________

- How I feel about our progress so far is:

____
____
____
____
____
____

- One thing I've learned about my adult/adults is:

____
____
____
____
____
____

- One thing I still need help with is:

____
____
____
____
____
____

SITUATION ________________________________

ADULT REFLECTION

- How I feel about our progress so far is:

___
___
___
___
___
___

- One thing I've learned about my kid is:

___
___
___
___
___
___

- One thing we can continue to work on is:

___
___
___
___
___
___

ADULT

SITUATION____

These words can sometimes be a bridge to opening up, making it easier to share feelings in a way that resonates. Circle a word, or words, that match your feelings currently. This helps who you're communicating with, know where you're coming from in your heart and mind.

Feel-Good Emotions:		**Hard-to-Discuss Feelings:**	
Grateful	Excited	Vulnerable	Resentful
Loved	Confident	Isolated	Unheard
Happy	Supported	Anxious	Trapped
Peaceful	Encouraged	Overwhelmed	Hopeless
Proud	Secure	Insecure	Lonely
Joyful	Hopeful	Misunderstood	Defeated
Appreciated	Inspired	Conflicted	Ashamed

Describe how you're feeling right now. Are you sad, angry, frustrated, worried, or something else? Write about why you're feeling this way.

I'm feeling:

____

____

____

____

____

____

____

____

____

What could my kid do to help?
Maybe you need them to listen, follow a rule, or talk calmly.

What I need from you is:

What things can you both do to solve the problem?
Maybe spend time talking, set up a new rule, or agree on a plan.

One thing we can do together to make things better is:

Do you need advice? **If so, what advice are you looking for?**

KID SITUATION_______________________________

These words can sometimes be a bridge to opening up, making it easier to share feelings in a way that resonates. Circle a word, or words, that match your feelings currently. This helps who you're communicating with, know where you're coming from in your heart and mind.

Feel-Good Emotions:		**Hard-to-Discuss Feelings:**	
Grateful	Excited	Vulnerable	Resentful
Loved	Confident	Isolated	Unheard
Happy	Supported	Anxious	Trapped
Peaceful	Encouraged	Overwhelmed	Hopeless
Proud	Secure	Insecure	Lonely
Joyful	Hopeful	Misunderstood	Defeated
Appreciated	Inspired	Conflicted	Ashamed

Describe how you're feeling right now. Are you sad, angry, frustrated, worried, or something else? Write about why you're feeling this way.

I'm feeling:

____

____

____

____

____

____

____

____

____

What could my adult do to help you feel better?
Maybe you need space, a hug, or just for them to listen.

What I need from you is:

____

____

____

____

____

____

____

____

What things can you both do to solve the problem?
Maybe spend time talking, set up a new rule, or agree on a plan.

One thing we can do together to make things better is:

____

Do you need advice? **If so, what advice are you looking for?**

____

____

____

____

____

____

____

____

KID REFLECTION SITUATION ______________________________

- How I feel about our progress so far is:

____
____
____
____
____
____

- One thing I've learned about my adult/adults is:

____
____
____
____
____
____

- One thing I still need help with is:

____
____
____
____
____
____

ADULT REFLECTION

SITUATION____

- How I feel about our progress so far is:

____

____

____

____

____

____

- One thing I've learned about my kid is:

____

____

____

____

____

____

- One thing we can continue to work on is:

____

____

____

____

____

____

ADULT SITUATION________________________________

These words can sometimes be a bridge to opening up, making it easier to share feelings in a way that resonates. Circle a word, or words, that match your feelings currently. This helps who you're communicating with, know where you're coming from in your heart and mind.

Feel-Good Emotions:		**Hard-to-Discuss Feelings:**	
Grateful	Excited	Vulnerable	Resentful
Loved	Confident	Isolated	Unheard
Happy	Supported	Anxious	Trapped
Peaceful	Encouraged	Overwhelmed	Hopeless
Proud	Secure	Insecure	Lonely
Joyful	Hopeful	Misunderstood	Defeated
Appreciated	Inspired	Conflicted	Ashamed

Describe how you're feeling right now. Are you sad, angry, frustrated, worried, or something else? Write about why you're feeling this way.

I'm feeling:

____

____

____

____

____

____

____

____

____

What could my kid do to help?
Maybe you need them to listen, follow a rule, or talk calmly.

What I need from you is:

____

____

____

____

____

____

____

____

____

What things can you both do to solve the problem?
Maybe spend time talking, set up a new rule, or agree on a plan.

One thing we can do together to make things better is:

____

Do you need advice? **If so, what advice are you looking for?**

____

____

____

____

____

____

____

KID SITUATION____________________

These words can sometimes be a bridge to opening up, making it easier to share feelings in a way that resonates. Circle a word, or words, that match your feelings currently. This helps who you're communicating with, know where you're coming from in your heart and mind.

Feel-Good Emotions:		**Hard-to-Discuss Feelings:**	
Grateful	Excited	Vulnerable	Resentful
Loved	Confident	Isolated	Unheard
Happy	Supported	Anxious	Trapped
Peaceful	Encouraged	Overwhelmed	Hopeless
Proud	Secure	Insecure	Lonely
Joyful	Hopeful	Misunderstood	Defeated
Appreciated	Inspired	Conflicted	Ashamed

Describe how you're feeling right now. Are you sad, angry, frustrated, worried, or something else? Write about why you're feeling this way.

I'm feeling:

____

____

____

____

____

____

____

____

____

What could my adult do to help you feel better?
Maybe you need space, a hug, or just for them to listen.

What I need from you is:

What things can you both do to solve the problem?
Maybe spend time talking, set up a new rule, or agree on a plan.

One thing we can do together to make things better is:

Do you need advice? **If so, what advice are you looking for?**

KID REFLECTION SITUATION________________________________

- How I feel about our progress so far is:

____

____

____

____

____

____

- One thing I've learned about my adult/adults is:

____

____

____

____

____

____

- One thing I still need help with is:

____

____

____

____

____

____

SITUATION____ **ADULT REFLECTION**

- How I feel about our progress so far is:

____

____

____

____

____

____

- One thing I've learned about my kid is:

____

____

____

____

____

____

- One thing we can continue to work on is:

____

____

____

____

____

____

ADULT SITUATION________________________________

These words can sometimes be a bridge to opening up, making it easier to share feelings in a way that resonates. Circle a word, or words, that match your feelings currently. This helps who you're communicating with, know where you're coming from in your heart and mind.

Feel-Good Emotions:		**Hard-to-Discuss Feelings:**	
Grateful	Excited	Vulnerable	Resentful
Loved	Confident	Isolated	Unheard
Happy	Supported	Anxious	Trapped
Peaceful	Encouraged	Overwhelmed	Hopeless
Proud	Secure	Insecure	Lonely
Joyful	Hopeful	Misunderstood	Defeated
Appreciated	Inspired	Conflicted	Ashamed

Describe how you're feeling right now. Are you sad, angry, frustrated, worried, or something else? Write about why you're feeling this way.

I'm feeling:

____

____

____

____

____

____

____

____

____

What could my kid do to help?
Maybe you need them to listen, follow a rule, or talk calmly.

What I need from you is:

What things can you both do to solve the problem?
Maybe spend time talking, set up a new rule, or agree on a plan.

One thing we can do together to make things better is:

Do you need advice? **If so, what advice are you looking for?**

KID SITUATION____

These words can sometimes be a bridge to opening up, making it easier to share feelings in a way that resonates. Circle a word, or words, that match your feelings currently. This helps who you're communicating with, know where you're coming from in your heart and mind.

Feel-Good Emotions:		Hard-to-Discuss Feelings:	
Grateful	Excited	Vulnerable	Resentful
Loved	Confident	Isolated	Unheard
Happy	Supported	Anxious	Trapped
Peaceful	Encouraged	Overwhelmed	Hopeless
Proud	Secure	Insecure	Lonely
Joyful	Hopeful	Misunderstood	Defeated
Appreciated	Inspired	Conflicted	Ashamed

Describe how you're feeling right now. Are you sad, angry, frustrated, worried, or something else? Write about why you're feeling this way.

I'm feeling:

____

____

____

____

____

____

____

____

____

What could my adult do to help you feel better?
Maybe you need space, a hug, or just for them to listen.

What I need from you is:

What things can you both do to solve the problem?
Maybe spend time talking, set up a new rule, or agree on a plan.

One thing we can do together to make things better is:

Do you need advice? **If so, what advice are you looking for?**

KID REFLECTION SITUATION ____________________

- How I feel about our progress so far is:

____

____

____

____

____

____

- One thing I've learned about my adult/adults is:

____

____

____

____

____

____

- One thing I still need help with is:

____

____

____

____

____

____

SITUATION____

ADULT REFLECTION

- How I feel about our progress so far is:

- One thing I've learned about my kid is:

- One thing we can continue to work on is:

ADULT SITUATION____

These words can sometimes be a bridge to opening up, making it easier to share feelings in a way that resonates. Circle a word, or words, that match your feelings currently. This helps who you're communicating with, know where you're coming from in your heart and mind.

Feel-Good Emotions:		Hard-to-Discuss Feelings:	
Grateful	Excited	Vulnerable	Resentful
Loved	Confident	Isolated	Unheard
Happy	Supported	Anxious	Trapped
Peaceful	Encouraged	Overwhelmed	Hopeless
Proud	Secure	Insecure	Lonely
Joyful	Hopeful	Misunderstood	Defeated
Appreciated	Inspired	Conflicted	Ashamed

Describe how you're feeling right now. Are you sad, angry, frustrated, worried, or something else? Write about why you're feeling this way.

I'm feeling:

____

____

____

____

____

____

____

____

____

What could my kid do to help?
Maybe you need them to listen, follow a rule, or talk calmly.

What I need from you is:

What things can you both do to solve the problem?
Maybe spend time talking, set up a new rule, or agree on a plan.

One thing we can do together to make things better is:

Do you need advice? **If so, what advice are you looking for?**

KID SITUATION____

These words can sometimes be a bridge to opening up, making it easier to share feelings in a way that resonates. Circle a word, or words, that match your feelings currently. This helps who you're communicating with, know where you're coming from in your heart and mind.

Feel-Good Emotions:		Hard-to-Discuss Feelings:	
Grateful	Excited	Vulnerable	Resentful
Loved	Confident	Isolated	Unheard
Happy	Supported	Anxious	Trapped
Peaceful	Encouraged	Overwhelmed	Hopeless
Proud	Secure	Insecure	Lonely
Joyful	Hopeful	Misunderstood	Defeated
Appreciated	Inspired	Conflicted	Ashamed

Describe how you're feeling right now. Are you sad, angry, frustrated, worried, or something else? Write about why you're feeling this way.

I'm feeling:

____

____

____

____

____

____

____

____

____

What could my adult do to help you feel better?
Maybe you need space, a hug, or just for them to listen.

What I need from you is:

What things can you both do to solve the problem?
Maybe spend time talking, set up a new rule, or agree on a plan.

One thing we can do together to make things better is:

Do you need advice? **If so, what advice are you looking for?**

KID REFLECTION

SITUATION ______________________

- How I feel about our progress so far is:

____

____

____

____

____

____

- One thing I've learned about my adult/adults is:

____

____

____

____

____

____

- One thing I still need help with is:

____

____

____

____

____

____

SITUATION____

ADULT REFLECTION

- How I feel about our progress so far is:

____

____

____

____

____

____

- One thing I've learned about my kid is:

____

____

____

____

____

____

- One thing we can continue to work on is:

____

____

____

____

____

____

ADULT SITUATION________________________________

These words can sometimes be a bridge to opening up, making it easier to share feelings in a way that resonates. Circle a word, or words, that match your feelings currently. This helps who you're communicating with, know where you're coming from in your heart and mind.

Feel-Good Emotions:		**Hard-to-Discuss Feelings:**	
Grateful	Excited	Vulnerable	Resentful
Loved	Confident	Isolated	Unheard
Happy	Supported	Anxious	Trapped
Peaceful	Encouraged	Overwhelmed	Hopeless
Proud	Secure	Insecure	Lonely
Joyful	Hopeful	Misunderstood	Defeated
Appreciated	Inspired	Conflicted	Ashamed

Describe how you're feeling right now. Are you sad, angry, frustrated, worried, or something else? Write about why you're feeling this way.

I'm feeling:

____

____

____

____

____

____

____

____

____

What could my kid do to help?
Maybe you need them to listen, follow a rule, or talk calmly.

What I need from you is:

What things can you both do to solve the problem?
Maybe spend time talking, set up a new rule, or agree on a plan.

One thing we can do together to make things better is:

Do you need advice? **If so, what advice are you looking for?**

KID SITUATION ______________________________

These words can sometimes be a bridge to opening up, making it easier to share feelings in a way that resonates. Circle a word, or words, that match your feelings currently. This helps who you're communicating with, know where you're coming from in your heart and mind.

Feel-Good Emotions:		**Hard-to-Discuss Feelings:**	
Grateful	Excited	Vulnerable	Resentful
Loved	Confident	Isolated	Unheard
Happy	Supported	Anxious	Trapped
Peaceful	Encouraged	Overwhelmed	Hopeless
Proud	Secure	Insecure	Lonely
Joyful	Hopeful	Misunderstood	Defeated
Appreciated	Inspired	Conflicted	Ashamed

Describe how you're feeling right now. Are you sad, angry, frustrated, worried, or something else? Write about why you're feeling this way.

I'm feeling:

____

____

____

____

____

____

____

____

____

What could my adult do to help you feel better?
Maybe you need space, a hug, or just for them to listen.

What I need from you is:

____

____

____

____

____

____

____

____

What things can you both do to solve the problem?
Maybe spend time talking, set up a new rule, or agree on a plan.

One thing we can do together to make things better is:

____

Do you need advice? **If so, what advice are you looking for?**

____

____

____

____

____

____

____

____

KID REFLECTION SITUATION ______________________________

- How I feel about our progress so far is:

____
____
____
____
____
____

- One thing I've learned about my adult/adults is:

____
____
____
____
____
____

- One thing I still need help with is:

____
____
____
____
____
____

SITUATION____

ADULT REFLECTION

- How I feel about our progress so far is:

____

____

____

____

____

____

- One thing I've learned about my kid is:

____

____

____

____

____

____

- One thing we can continue to work on is:

____

____

____

____

____

____

ADULT SITUATION________________________________

These words can sometimes be a bridge to opening up, making it easier to share feelings in a way that resonates. Circle a word, or words, that match your feelings currently. This helps who you're communicating with, know where you're coming from in your heart and mind.

Feel-Good Emotions:		Hard-to-Discuss Feelings:	
Grateful	Excited	Vulnerable	Resentful
Loved	Confident	Isolated	Unheard
Happy	Supported	Anxious	Trapped
Peaceful	Encouraged	Overwhelmed	Hopeless
Proud	Secure	Insecure	Lonely
Joyful	Hopeful	Misunderstood	Defeated
Appreciated	Inspired	Conflicted	Ashamed

Describe how you're feeling right now. Are you sad, angry, frustrated, worried, or something else? Write about why you're feeling this way.

I'm feeling:

____

____

____

____

____

____

____

____

____

What could my kid do to help?
Maybe you need them to listen, follow a rule, or talk calmly.

What I need from you is:

What things can you both do to solve the problem?
Maybe spend time talking, set up a new rule, or agree on a plan.

One thing we can do together to make things better is:

Do you need advice? **If so, what advice are you looking for?**

KID SITUATION____________________________________

These words can sometimes be a bridge to opening up, making it easier to share feelings in a way that resonates. Circle a word, or words, that match your feelings currently. This helps who you're communicating with, know where you're coming from in your heart and mind.

Feel-Good Emotions:		**Hard-to-Discuss Feelings:**	
Grateful	Excited	Vulnerable	Resentful
Loved	Confident	Isolated	Unheard
Happy	Supported	Anxious	Trapped
Peaceful	Encouraged	Overwhelmed	Hopeless
Proud	Secure	Insecure	Lonely
Joyful	Hopeful	Misunderstood	Defeated
Appreciated	Inspired	Conflicted	Ashamed

Describe how you're feeling right now. Are you sad, angry, frustrated, worried, or something else? Write about why you're feeling this way.

I'm feeling:

____

____

____

____

____

____

____

____

____

What could my adult do to help you feel better?
Maybe you need space, a hug, or just for them to listen.

What I need from you is:

What things can you both do to solve the problem?
Maybe spend time talking, set up a new rule, or agree on a plan.

One thing we can do together to make things better is:

Do you need advice? **If so, what advice are you looking for?**

KID REFLECTION

SITUATION____

- How I feel about our progress so far is:

____

____

____

____

____

____

- One thing I've learned about my adult/adults is:

____

____

____

____

____

____

- One thing I still need help with is:

____

____

____

____

____

____

SITUATION____

ADULT REFLECTION

- How I feel about our progress so far is:

____

____

____

____

____

____

- One thing I've learned about my kid is:

____

____

____

____

____

____

- One thing we can continue to work on is:

____

____

____

____

____

____

ADULT SITUATION____

These words can sometimes be a bridge to opening up, making it easier to share feelings in a way that resonates. Circle a word, or words, that match your feelings currently. This helps who you're communicating with, know where you're coming from in your heart and mind.

Feel-Good Emotions:		**Hard-to-Discuss Feelings:**	
Grateful	Excited	Vulnerable	Resentful
Loved	Confident	Isolated	Unheard
Happy	Supported	Anxious	Trapped
Peaceful	Encouraged	Overwhelmed	Hopeless
Proud	Secure	Insecure	Lonely
Joyful	Hopeful	Misunderstood	Defeated
Appreciated	Inspired	Conflicted	Ashamed

Describe how you're feeling right now. Are you sad, angry, frustrated, worried, or something else? Write about why you're feeling this way.

I'm feeling:

____

____

____

____

____

____

____

____

____

What could my kid do to help?
Maybe you need them to listen, follow a rule, or talk calmly.

What I need from you is:

What things can you both do to solve the problem?
Maybe spend time talking, set up a new rule, or agree on a plan.

One thing we can do together to make things better is:

Do you need advice? **If so, what advice are you looking for?**

KID SITUATION________________________________

These words can sometimes be a bridge to opening up, making it easier to share feelings in a way that resonates. Circle a word, or words, that match your feelings currently. This helps who you're communicating with, know where you're coming from in your heart and mind.

Feel-Good Emotions:		**Hard-to-Discuss Feelings:**	
Grateful	Excited	Vulnerable	Resentful
Loved	Confident	Isolated	Unheard
Happy	Supported	Anxious	Trapped
Peaceful	Encouraged	Overwhelmed	Hopeless
Proud	Secure	Insecure	Lonely
Joyful	Hopeful	Misunderstood	Defeated
Appreciated	Inspired	Conflicted	Ashamed

Describe how you're feeling right now. Are you sad, angry, frustrated, worried, or something else? Write about why you're feeling this way.

I'm feeling:

____

____

____

____

____

____

____

____

____

What could my adult do to help you feel better?
Maybe you need space, a hug, or just for them to listen.

What I need from you is:

____

____

____

____

____

____

____

____

What things can you both do to solve the problem?
Maybe spend time talking, set up a new rule, or agree on a plan.

One thing we can do together to make things better is:

____

Do you need advice? **If so, what advice are you looking for?**

____

____

____

____

____

____

____

____

KID REFLECTION SITUATION________________________________

- How I feel about our progress so far is:

____

____

____

____

____

____

- One thing I've learned about my adult/adults is:

____

____

____

____

____

____

- One thing I still need help with is:

____

____

____

____

____

____

SITUATION ____

ADULT REFLECTION

- How I feel about our progress so far is:

____
____
____
____
____
____

- One thing I've learned about my kid is:

____
____
____
____
____
____

- One thing we can continue to work on is:

____
____
____
____
____
____

> “The art of conversation is the art of hearing as well as of being heard.”
>
> —William Hazlitt

THOUGHTS FROM THE AUTHOR

I created this adult-kid communication journal with a vision of changing family dynamics and reshaping the generational tree for years to come, helping families build lasting bonds. When I look back, I often wish there were written memories of conversations with my parents—guidance, understanding, or even the tough talks—something tangible that captured those connections. If we had those words on paper, they'd be a precious keepsake, something to pass down, offering comfort and wisdom even after loved ones are no longer with us.

Growing up, communication was often a one-way street. In my era, we were taught to listen, obey, and follow the rules set by those older than us, no questions asked. Even when I felt differently, it was hard to express myself without fear of getting in trouble or being misunderstood. Many times, I stayed silent to avoid conflict, holding in my feelings because I worried how my honesty might affect others. Looking back, I wish I had a way to share my truth safely and build a relationship where we could truly understand each other.

This journal is meant to provide just that—a safe space where everyone in the family can be heard and respected, a place for honesty, understanding, and support. Sometimes, writing helps us express what we can't easily say. It allows us to share emotions, dreams, and worries in a way that feels safe and open, breaking down barriers that words alone can't.

My hope is that this journal will give you and your family a new experience, one of deep connection and mutual growth. By committing to this journey together, you're creating a foundation of love and understanding that will not only impact your family but ripple out to your community and beyond. This small act of writing and sharing can be a powerful step toward reducing conflict, fostering empathy, and building stronger bonds at home and beyond. I welcome you to lean all the way in, connect fully, support one another, and help each other grow.

“

Sometimes you will never know the value of a moment until it becomes a memory.

—Dr. Seuss

”

KEEPSAKE

This section is designed to be so much more than just a place to write things down. It's a treasure chest of memories, dreams, and shared experiences that will only grow in meaning over the years.

Each page is a special space for you and your kid to create memories, have fun, and build a family bond that can last a lifetime. By taking the time to fill in these sections together, you're creating a keepsake that captures who you are, what you love, and what you hope for—something you'll both cherish forever.

These pages aren't just for filling out—they're for coming back to again and again. Each entry adds to a keepsake that will remind you of your journey together, the laughter, the dreams, and all the little moments in between.

1. Bucket List Brainstorm:

Dream big together! This is where you and your kid can create a bucket list of all the things you want to do together—from big trips like "see the Northern Lights" to small adventures like "have a camp out in the backyard." This page is for dreaming as a team. Every time you look back on this list, it'll be a reminder of your shared hopes and goals.

2. Invention Ideas:

Have fun imagining and creating! Fill this section with your wildest ideas, like a "homework-doing robot" or "a device to find each other at concerts." Let your imagination run free! By dreaming up inventions, you're showing each other how dreams can start as ideas and then grow into reality with teamwork.

3. Travel Destinations:

What places do you want to experience together? Use this space to write down destinations and set goals for when you'll visit them—before age 10, 18, or even just "someday soon." This page will be a map of the journeys you want to take, each one a reminder of the world you plan to explore side by side.

4. Secret Handshake Tutorial:

Design a handshake that's just for the two of you! Write out each move, give them silly names, and have fun practicing. Every time you use this handshake, it'll remind you of the time you spent creating it and the special connection you have—something uniquely yours to keep forever.

5. Favorites Tracker:

Capture your favorite things in this section—books, movies, foods, or songs. Over the years, you'll see how tastes change, and you'll be able to look back and laugh or reminisce over those shared favorites. This section will always be a snapshot of who you both were in that moment.

6. "Dear Me" Letter-KID:

Write letters to your future selves. What do you hope for? What dreams do you have? Write one-year, five-year, or even ten-year letters to yourselves. When you read these later, you'll see how much you've both grown and what goals came true, making this a powerful time capsule of your hopes and growth.

7. "Dear Me" Letter-ADULT:

Write letters to your future selves. What do you hope for? What dreams do you have? Write one-year, five-year, or even ten-year letters to yourselves. When you read these later, you'll see how much you've both grown and what goals came true, making this a powerful time capsule of your hopes and growth.

8. Dreams & Goals Page:

Write down your dreams and goals, big and small. As you cheer each other on and check in over time, this space becomes a record of encouragement and support. Each goal you add brings you closer as a team and shows how much you believe in each other.

9.

Gratitude List:

What are three things you're thankful for in your life?

- Example: "1. Mom making my favorite breakfast. 2. My friend Joey. 3. Having clean food and water."

10. Joke of the Year:

Each person writes a joke for the other to read. This keepsake will be remembered forever when you or someone else reads this in the future. Reveal how funny you are here, or how corny you are.

- Example: "Why did the scarecrow win an award? Because he was outstanding in his field!"